Johnny's Song

JOHNNY'S SONG

Steve Mason

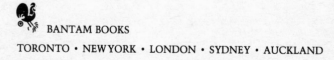
BANTAM BOOKS

TORONTO · NEW YORK · LONDON · SYDNEY · AUCKLAND

JOHNNY'S SONG
A Bantam Book / May 1986

Library of Congress Cataloging-in-Publication Data

Mason, Steve.
  Johnny's song.

  I. Title.
PS3563.A798J6 1986   811'.54   85-48232
ISBN 0-553-05160-1

Published simultaneously in the United States and Canada

PRINTED IN THE UNITED STATES OF AMERICA

MV   0 9 8 7 6 5 4 3 2 1

Dedicated
to all of us
who know the true cost
of war
and have paid the price. . . .

Contents

THE WALL WITHIN

Delivered at the commencement of the National Salute II in Washington, D.C., on November 10, 1984, as part of the official activities prior to the dedication of the Vietnam Veterans Memorial ("The Wall") as a national monument. It honors the personal list of love and loss that each American has marked in his/her heart. Poem entered into the Congressional Record, January 30, 1985.

THE WALL WITHIN

Most real men
hanging tough
in their early forties
would like the rest of us to think
they could really handle one more war
and two more women.
But I know better.
You have no more lies to tell.
I have no more dreams to believe.

I have seen it in your face
I am sure you have noticed it
in mine;
that thousand-yard stare
that does not look out—
it looks in—
at the unutterable,
unalterable truth of our war.

The eye sees
what the mind believes.
And all that I know of war,
all that I have heard of peace,
has me looking over my shoulder
for that one bullet
which still has my name on it—
circling
round and round the globe
waiting and circling
circling and waiting
until I break from cover
and it takes its best, last shot.
In the absence of Time,
the accuracy of guilt is assured.
It is a cosmic marksman.

Since Vietnam,
I have run a zigzag course
across the open fields of America
taking refuge in the inner cities.
From MacArthur Park
to Washington Square
from Centennial Park
to DuPont Circle,
on the grassy, urban knolls of America
I have seen an army of combat veterans
hidden among the trees.
Veterans of all our recent wars.
Each a part of the best of his generation.
Waiting in his teeth for peace.

They do not lurk there
on the backs of park benches
drooling into their socks
above the remote, turtled backs
of chessplayers playing soldiers.
They do not perch upon the gutter's lip
of midnight fountains
and noontime wishing wells
like surrealistic gargoyles
guarding the coins and simple wishes
of young lovers.
No.
I have seen them in the quiet dignity
of their aloneness.
Singly, in the confidence
of their own perspective.
And always at the edges of the clearing.
Patrolling like perimeter guards,
or observing as primitive gods,
each in his own way looks out to the park
that he might "see" in to the truth.

Some, like me
enjoy the comfortable base
of a friendly tree
that we might cock one eye
to the center of the park
toward the rearing bronze horsemen
of other wars
who would lead us backwards to glory.
Daily, they are fragged
by a platoon of disgruntled pigeons
saying it best for all of us.

And with the other eye,
we read the poetry of America the Beautiful
as she combs her midday hair
and eats precise shrimp sandwiches
and salad Niçoise catered by Tupperware—
and never leaves a single crumb.
No wonder America is the only country
in the world which doesn't smell like food.

. . . and I remember you and me
picnicking at the side
of the Ho Chi Minh Trail in the rain
eating the Limas and Ham from the can
sitting easy in our youth and our strength
driving hard bargains with each other
for the C-ration goodies
we unwrapped like Christmas presents.
Somehow it really seemed to matter
what he got versus what you got.

6

It wasn't easy trading cheese and crackers
for chocolate-covered peanut butter cookies!
And the pound cake—Forget about it!
I knew a guy would cut a hole in it
and pretend it was a doughnut.
For six months I watched that
and refused to ask him about it.
I did finally. And you guessed it.
He hated pound cake.
And remember the water biscuit
that came in its own tin?—
I think they had the moxie to call it a cookie—
it came with the marmalade
and was made by that outfit in Chicago
we promised to burn to the ground someday.
Damn, how did your buddy, the animal,
ever eat that crap?
Then, we'd happily wash down the whole mess
with freckly-faced strawberry Kool-Aid
straight from the canteen
some days there'd be goofy grape
(anything to keep from choking
on the taste of purified water).
Bleck.
But somehow I sensed all the while
that I'd never be able to forgive myself
for enjoying your company so much
or being so good at the game we played.

We were the best—You & I.

In our parks,
there are whole other armies of veterans
mostly young and mostly old
but always ageless
who are not alone.
They share with their families
and their friends
these open-aired
above-ground time capsules
of our national culture.
They read aloud to themselves
and their children
from the plaques and statues
monuments and markers
those one-line truths
of our common experience
as if there could be a real significance
in words like Love and Hate tatooed
on the clenched, granite fists of America.

Sometimes, when I am angry
it seems as if I could start my own country
with the same twenty Spill and Spell words
we shake out at the feet of our heroes
like some crone spreading her hands
over the runes prior to a mystic reading.
Words like:
peace and sacrifice, war and young
supreme and duty, service and honor
country, nation, men and men and men again,
sometimes God and don't forget women!
Army, Air Force, Navy, Marines and freedom.

Then, just as quickly, the anger passes
and reverence takes its place.
Those are good words, noble words, solemn
   & sincere.
It is the language of Death
which frightens me;
it is unearthly to speak life concepts
over the dead.
Death is inarticulately final
refusing forever to negotiate.

That, and the awesome responsibility
we place eternally on our fallen
teenage sons,
seems unbearably heavy
against the lengthening, prancing
shadows of Sunday's frisbeers.

Apparently, there is no period
which can be placed after sacrifice.
All life is struggle.
An act of natural balance
and indomitable courage.
As it is with man
so it is with mankind.

If we permit Memorial Day
to come to us every day,
we ignore the concept of sacrifice
and dilute its purpose.
When we do that
we incur the responsibility
to effect change.
If we are successful,
the sacrifice has renewed meaning.
It seems there is no alternative to life.
But there may be to war . . .

The values of our society
seem to be distributed in our parks
and reflected in the eyes of veterans
who look there for validation
and find only confusion and sadness.
Strange, I have observed no monuments
to survivors.
No obelisk to mark the conflict
of those who risked
and lived perhaps to fight again
or perhaps to speak of peace.
Nowhere, yet, a wall for the living.
There is no wonder
guilt is the sole survivor of war.
We do not celebrate life after combat
because our concept of glory
lives neither in victory nor in peace
but in Death.

There are plaques at the doorsteps
of skyscrapers;
in New York on 10th and the Avenue
of the Americas it reads:

IN MEMORY OF THOSE
FROM
GREENWICH VILLAGE
WHO MADE THE SUPREME SACRIFICE
IN THE KOREAN CONFLICT

1950–1953

In Nashville's Centennial Park
in a shaded wood
to one side of the Parthenon
built to scale and to the glory
which was Greece,
a small statue stands;
it is inscribed:

I GAVE MY BEST
TO MAKE A BETTER WORLD

1917–1918

I stood there one fall
ankle deep in leaves
and looked up at the night sky
through a hole in a ceiling of trees
wondering how much better the world
might look from up there.

From the moon
only one manmade object
can be viewed by the naked eye:
The Great Wall of China
(a tribute to man's functional paranoia).
It's a peculiar perspective
because we're a lot closer
and the only manmade object We can see
is THE Wall in Washington, D.C.
(the veterans' solemn pledge to remember)

There is one other wall, of course.
One we never speak of.
One we never see,
One which separates memory from madness.
In a place no one offers flowers.
THE WALL WITHIN.
We permit no visitors.

Mine looks like any of a million
nameless, brick walls—
it stands in the tear-down ghetto of my soul;
that part of me which reason avoids
for fear of dirtying its clothes
and from atop which my sorrow and my rage
hurl bottles and invectives
at the rolled-up windows
of my passing youth.

Do you know the wall I mean?

I learned of mine that night in the rain
when I spoke at the Memorial in Washington.
We all noticed how the wall ran like tears
and every man's name we found
on the polished, black granite face
seemed to have our eyes staring back at us;
crying.
It was haunting.
Later I would realize
I had caught my first glimpse
of the Wall Within.
And those tears were real.

You and I do not walk about the Wall Within
like Hamlet on the battlements.
No one with our savvy
would expose himself like that
especially to a frightened, angry man.
Suicide loiters in our subconscious
and bears a grudge; an assassin
on hashish. We must be wary.
No. We sit there legless in our immobility
rolling precariously in our self-pity
like ugly Humpty Dumpties
with disdain even for the King's horses
as we lean over the ledge to write
upside down with chalk, bleached white
with our truth
the names of all the other casualties
of the Vietnam War
(our loved ones)

the ones the Pentagon didn't put in uniform
but died anyway.
Some because they stopped being who
they always were
just as truly as if they'd found
another way to breathe.
Others, because they did die
honest-to-God casualties of the
Vietnam War
because they lost the will
to breathe at all.

My mother gave her first recital
at Carnegie Hall at age eleven.
Sometimes, when I was a boy
I'd watch her play the piano
and wonder if God, after all, was not a woman.
One evening when I was in the bush
she turned on the 6:00 news
and died of a heart attack.

My mother's name is on the Wall Within.

You starting to get the idea?
Our lists may be different
but shoulder to shoulder
if we could find the right flat cloud
on a perfect, black night
we could project our images
upon a god-sized drive-in theatre
wide enough to race Ben Hur across
for a thousand years . . .

Because the Wall Within
adds up the true cost of war . . .

We can recite 58,012 in our sleep
even the day after they update it,
but how many of those KIA had kids?
How many of them got nice step-dads?
Whose wall do they go on?

And what about you vets
who came home to your wife and kids
only to divorce her because
there wasn't anybody else to be angry at?
How many dimes
have you long-distance fathers
dropped into the slot
to hear how another man
was raising your children?
Yeah, Yeah, I can hear you hollerin',
"Put it on the wall! Put it on the wall!"
Damn right, it's on the wall . . .
And you remember how that came down?
You told the three year old
his daddy loved him
and his mommy loved him
and nothing would ever change that.
But it did anyway.
But not because you didn't love him enough,
but because you loved him too much
to be a part-time daddy.
And you couldn't explain that to him

because you couldn't explain it to you.
What the hell? I mean who were you,
Spinoza? You came home a twenty-two-year-old
machine gunner for chrissake,
you did the best you could.

PUT IT ON THE WALL!!

And somewhere, in an art gallery, maybe,
is a portrait of American Grieving Parenthood.
Handholding, Rockwellian caricatures
of wisdom and forbearance
and oh yes, pride
sitting on the front porch
of the township
waving their lemonades
at the Greyhound bus driver.
Baloney. The names go UP!
Because every time you can't find Mom,
you damned well better call Doc Smith
'cause she's up on the second floor again
sitting on the floor in Johnny's closet
smelling his Varsity sweater
with the sleeves around her shoulders
sobbing something maybe only Johnny ever
understood.

But don't worry about dad,
who never fished again,
or watched a ballgame on TV again
and won't talk to anyone this year
between the ages of thirty and forty.
He's doing fine.
He just doesn't exercise
as much as he should,
but Doc Smith assures us there's no medical
reason why the folks should have
separate bedrooms;
Dad just likes to read a lot these days.

If you and I were men of common conscience
we might agree on a collective dedication
to our Walls Within.
As for me
they could all read:
This wall is dedicated
to mothers, fathers, sisters, brothers,
wives, husbands,
sons, daughters,
lovers, friends
and most of all dreams
of the men and women
who risked it all in Vietnam
while you continued to lose them
during and after the war
with less a chance than they for a parade
and no chance at all for an explanation.

You lost them to bullets, internment,
drugs, suicide, alcohol, jail, PTS,
Divorce, but never never did any of you
ever lose them to the truth
which is now being shared
across this great nation
in such an act of spontaneous
moral courage, its like may never
have been seen on any battlefield
in the history of mankind . . .

Amen to that, brother.

DEROS: MY SOUL

This poem speaks to the many men and women who have experienced the anxiety of still being in Vietnam—of not having completely returned to the world of which they no longer feel an integral part.

Note—DEROS is a military term meaning "date of expected return from overseas."

DEROS: My Soul

I.

At times when I am calm
I remember
that even if you waited for it
nothing came as suddenly
as gunfire
and nothing (not even the Lieutenant)
seemed as stupid
as the silence that followed—

At such times I know also
that each of us
who fought in Vietnam
was spiritually captured by it
and that each remains
a prisoner
of his own war—

It is, therefore, not surprising
that for some (like for me)
the AfterNam emptiness
published no DEROS
for the soul . . .

Yet, in moments better known to me
when reason drifts
and whole worlds are illuminated
with Platonic images
dancing against the cave-walls
of my mind
lit by a single candle
borrowed from a twilight wish,
I take the stairs two at a time
and wait in the second-floor window
of my days
hoping that Someday will come next morning
and that I'll recognize the soul
of a much younger me
come diddily-bopping up the street
eating a Sky Bar
and hefting a duffle bag
filled with new and more believable myths
that I might live by
(not to mention back pay)
while humming something (in a nasal sort of way)
about going to San Francisco
and something else I can't make out
about a flower in somebody's hair—

Frankly, I don't know if I'd throw flowers
or run down stairs, meet him at the curb
and beat Hell out of him—
leaving me the way he did!

You know, there never was any great debate
(between my soul and me)
ending in a mutually agreed upon
existential parting of the ways.

I mean it's not like my damned soul
dressed up like a teensy-weensy
Jennifer Jones in drag
and waved farewell with a lace hanky
from the base of a bonsai plant
in a Tu do Street floral shop
while I dreamt too soundly
on Ba Muy Ba beer and woke next morning
to discover
I couldn't cry anymore
or laugh like before
or give a shit period—

And my soul didn't just go berserk
under the too bright light
of a Government Moon
and go roaring down Highway 1
doing a wheely on a cycilo
like James Dean in a steel pot
and flak jacket
laughing a Red Baron kind of laugh
and quoting Kipling's Barrack-Room Ballads—

No.

My soul just did
what most souls did.
Just disappeared one afternoon
when I was in a firefight.
Just "walked away" in the scuffle
like a Dunhill lighter
off the deck of a redneck bar . . .

II.

Peculiar,
A man can lose his money
his woman
(even his mind)
and still he can come back,
but if he loses his courage
or his pride
then—
it is over . . .

And what of a lost soul?
(I ask myself)
when madness invades
scattering today's headlines
like March Hares
leaving nothing at the table
of my reason
beyond one crumb of truth
and the enormous bloodstain
on the white cloth of my youth—
shaped

(if you come 'round this side
of the table & cock your head
just so)
like a distorted lunar projection
of Vietnam—
And careful! Don't strike your knee
against that table leg!
'Cause then it jumps alive—
like somebody flunked
the inkblot test
and knocking over the candelabra
dives out the window of my sanity
to run naked down the street
lined on both sides by
Vietnam Vets
who couldn't sleep either
and just followed the blood trail
like mute somnambulists
in a black and white foreign film
because they heard that tonight
their shared nightmare
(with Vietnamese subtitles)
had called a muster of lost souls
to be followed by Nam,
Bloody Nam,
leading a one-man parade
and twirling a baton
that looked like nobody's penis
I ever saw
and probably belonged
to the guy in back of me
(poor bastard)—

Geez, it gets scary in here sometimes,
do it not, Brutha?
And oooh, Sister! Do *you* have songs to sing?!
About war without glory
and love beyond reward . . .

Maybe someday God will mint a medal
so beautiful, no words are printed on it
and all of our sisters
who were there with us
would get one
and everyone, everywhere, who saw it
would know just what it was
and would find a "thoughtful place"
to go sit down in for a week—

And then maybe God would let us have
a picnic (bigger than the moon)
and all the boys and girls
of daddies whose lives they saved
could hold hands
to make a daisy chain for the sun.
And when it was all done
the big people
would make God a prayer-promise
never, never to do anything like Nam
again.
And when the cheers died down
the sun would bow his head
(ever so slightly)
so the children might wish their necklace

'round his head
and when it was in place,
all of a sudden—
faster, even than gunfire,
everybody's lost soul
would just come floating down
like a bright balloon
on a string
and mine
(the smart-assed red one)
would wink at yours
and pretend not to see me
and when everyone got his,
All the children would sing
Happy Birthday! Happy Birthday!
over and over and over again
until all the ice cream melted
and all
our hearts . . .

THE LAST PATROL

Some survive by blocking the past. Others by working through it. For the combat veteran of Vietnam, reliving a critical moment in his war can become all too real. Even the smells come back. . . .

THE LAST PATROL

In my neighborhood (when I was a kid)
we didn't know how to cure it,
but we knew how you *got* it,
"Walk around all day
in your wet bathing suit
and you'll get Polio!"
That's it—
We were ahead of the scientists
by about eight years!
Jeez, we were smart.

We also knew how to avoid
the second most dreaded injury
in the whole world,
"Don't pick that up by yourself!
You'll get a HERNIA!!!
or worse—the unspeakable
DOUBLE (cross yourself) HERNIA!!!
AARGH"
Forget about that no one
ever knew anybody who had one
(or both)

it was enough that grandmothers
shrieked against them—
and if They shrieked
We listened.

Funny thing about that neighborhood,
we always asked about the kids
you know, years later
like, "Whatever happened to that
Irish kid, Tommy? Ya' know the one
I mean could hitta ball
to fuckin' Mars
an' run like a deer—Phizzz,
he was fast . . ."
—He got killed in Korea.

"An ya' rememba' da' Feinstein kid?
Da' one wit da' tradin' cards?
Always flippin' always tradin'
'Super Flipper' he usta call himself . . .
Brudda' was a big wheel on da' Exchange?"
—Lieutenant Feinstein MIA in Vietnam.

Funny thing about my neighborhood,
we knew so much about so many things
and mainly about how to love life
(the secret was in sharing yours).
But we didn't know jack-shit
about keeping our kids safe from war—
forget about that we didn't even know
anybody who ever found anything good
in one . . .

Maybe that's why our grandmothers
shrieked so much when we left.
And maybe we shoulda listened.

Like you,
I was raised
in the centerfield of summer,
in a time
when everybody's grandmother
was still alive
and kids and weeds grew
only to keep baseballs from bouncing
into another world—
It was pure and good
and unfortunately not real,
but it was sweet enough
to last a lifetime
as every boyhood should . . .

For us, it began
with fourth-grade dreams
of long home runs
and loud applause
and ended (for some of us)
when they moved
Jackie Robinson
off second base
never to return
from left field—

I knew right away
something very big
was very wrong
with my little world.

Later, that summer
there was a death
in the family,
but I had already been prepared.

For most of us, though
the "game" ended
behind a locked bathroom door
just down the road from boyhood
about a hundred yards
from the end of the earth
where parallel lines meet
and the concepts of toys and sex
collide
in increasingly frequent,
fantastic visits
(lasting longer than a double-header)
and eventually causing
the dissolution of more secret pacts
among the many alliances of youth
than the surrender
of Nazi Germany— Girls, Yuk!

There, on that very spot
(about a block and half
from the Plains of Runnymede)
Hermes sewed the Levi Tag
into the butt seam of the world
as a monument to the end
of baggy boyhood
and the incessant
between-the-teeth whistlings
of "the very young at heart."

And Johnny's Song begins . . .

Johnny's Song (I call it)
the song of each man's soul
who has come from a boyhood
such as ours
and gone to a war
such as we have known
and as yet has no DEROS.

I would gladly put it to words
and play it for you
(if only I could) on a flute,
but what the hell,
you know it by heart anyway . . .

I heard it once
somewhere between the finite
mathematics of harmony
and the infinitely inescapable
possibilities of loneliness.
Heard it, in the sad music
of solitary whales
in the North Atlantic
and recognized the voice
of my own soul
swimming also
in the dark
in the cold
under the implacable pull of the moon.

When a man is lost
he returns to the last known thing—
It is possible the same is true
for souls.
I have rummaged, therefore,
through childhood
for the essence of my manhood
and the substance of my humanity.
I have found only where the boy
was born—and where he learned
to trust and to love,
but since I am no longer he,
it becomes a vague exercise
like viewing the cosmos
through a kaleidoscope
(delightful, but without value).

A lot of good men died in Vietnam.
But like some of you, I was born there.
So sometimes (like you)
I just get tired of waiting for me
to feel like me again
and on days like that—
late nights actually
(the days after Nam
have always come and gone
like meaningless ricochets)
I just pull back the final perimeter
of my fat and bivouacked-by-the-fire
middle age
to the very edge of the TV,
hunker down into the chair
and get black-faced in my mind
(and blank in my heart)
ready to slip under the wire
for one last patrol.

And with the last strains
of the "Star Spangled Banner"
in my ears
the tube turns the night into snow
and I am gone—
Quietly,
quickly,
past the concertina
on the downward slope
of my nightly fears

into the no man's land
from which my instinct draws
the knowledge to explain
(in dream symbols) all I failed to see
when first I lived it.

Tonight I am moving smoothly
(even in my pain)
and I am missing nothing—
I am a one man
search and recollect mission.

Back. Way Back, the way I came in.
And this time maybe I'll find it.
Whatever "it" was that went wrong.
Christ, it could be something
obvious that was there all along—
like being party to the least
experienced group of combat soldiers
ever sent into combat.
Some killers we showed up to be!
Of the nearly three million guys
"in country"
probably eighteen of us killed chickens
for lunch down on the farm—
one hundred and twelve
caught fish in a stocked pond
(big enough to keep)
and the rest of us manicured killers
let the likes of Burger Chef
do our bludgeoning for us.

Really, did you ever kill a chicken?
I never killed a chicken. Shit.
Where I come from kill a chicken
spend the rest of your life
in reform school. It was like a jingle.
I never killed anything.
First thing I ever killed
was no kind of thing at all—
it was an enemy soldier
which is a hell of a lot easier
to say than
the first thing I ever killed
was a man.

See that? Back to childhood again.
How unprepared for real life
we were.
I've got a sister forty years old
I don't think to this day
my father has the heart to tell her
pork chops come from l'l piggies.

Damn! I go off to war and what do I get
in my bag of tricks from childhood?
What is it I tap into in crisis?
Thirteen Ralph Kiners
Triples in the entire starting lineup
of the 1952 Brooklyn Dodgers
and the top half of the
game winning Spalding Hi-Bouncer
that warped off the end of my stick

into a dreaded "egg-ball"
that was so vicious
that when poor Dumb-Eddie
clamped his mitts on it—it split
(and the run scored).

Pretty tame stuff
compared to Madam Tich's
little boy, Nguyen, anyway
who came to kill me one afternoon
in the Plain of Reeds
(not near Runnymede)
and brought his own duck with him
as an appetizer
(strung upside down from his belt).

And oh, oh there it is!
Careful, just like it was real life
step over those same trip wires
like the first time.
Can I screw up? Can I blow myself up
in a late-night reverie
(a little on the frantic side)?
Can I change the past
and be dead all along? Oh, shit:
And there's the pagoda
where I drop my Zippo
and bend to pick it up
as the rounds hit the wall above me
like freight trains
and I become the first guy in history
who can say cigarette smoking
saved his life . . .

I am moving even better now
and my guts tell me
that in these next moments
I will be reunited with myself
in that irrevocable moment of truth
when last my mind and body, heart and soul
were as one . . .
There it is, the church in the rain
(on this side of the canal from Cambodia).
On both sides
the flood rises
the war worsens
and the monsoons are no more interested
than typhus or the plague,
Through the storm the church looks
like a shadow
and in my mind it has ever remained so.
That night, when we were ambushed,
I was certain it was the only building
left standing between Kien Phong Province
and Augusta, Georgia.

When he woke up next morning,
Nguyen must have weighed 90 lbs.
(I could have killed him
with my bad breath)
instead somebody shot him 5 times
(the duck they missed completely).
When he crawled out of the water
to die on the thick mud outside
the church door

(the flood left little room)
I had just left the church
preferring the rain and the danger
to the roistering inside
where cooking fires had been started
and men rode each other's shoulders
to drape the wet clothing
over the support beams,
pitifully decorated with faded
pink crepe paper
scalloped and twisted by some long gone
custodian of the faith.
After several sharp words from me
they reluctantly gave up the torture
of two hapless captives
and as I turned to leave I noticed
that the dais was covered
with flat sheets of uncut
French grape soda cans
and on the podium an erect
decapitated statuette of Christ stood
(the head placed gently at the base).

Outside I sensed Nguyen's presence
before I saw him
almost directly
at my feet;
Even in the rain
and the faint light of the church
his wounds were atrocious.
I sat with him in the mud

and put a soggy cigarette in his lips
to allay his fears of me
and stroked his hair,
"Toi com biet," (I don't understand)
he whimpered.
I was silent.
He was in unbearable pain.
He moved his head with great effort
(and even greater meaning)
to the pistol at my side.

Back inside the church
the muffled "puff"
which blew Nguyen's lights out
was barely discernible
above the rain
(but for me it still echoes).

I stopped by the dais
and spoke directly
to the Christ head,
"Toi com biet."
Arms at my side
I turned into the laughter
of the smoke-filled room
into the gold, gap-toothed smile
of a little man with a big knife
holding Nguyen's duck over his head
like a trophy—
raising my head to the rafters
I howled like a mad dog,
"ANYBODY FOR A LITTLE STICKBALL!?"

A HISTORY LESSON

Written in the Biltmore Hotel in Los Angeles following a week-long, joint convention of two national historical societies. Their treatment of the Vietnam War prompted this poem.

A HISTORY LESSON

Since Vietnam,
three things
hold my universe together:
gravity, centrifugal force
and guilt.

It is not so strange, therefore,
that the war is over for me
just like it's over for you.
Over.
And
over
again . . .

There remains no resolution of this war
beyond each man's obligation
to his world and his conscience
to record the True inner-history
of his Vietnam experience.

Scholars believe it is too soon
for a history of what I call
the "outer war"
perhaps it is too soon also
for the "inner war"
but I doubt it—
for ours is not a justifiable history
to be recorded in reasonable terms—
ours, not a conflict involved
in economics or politics
militarism or religious crusade.
No. Our war is a moral one.
One to be agonized, not written.
One which must be shared,
not taught.
Ours, too honest a lesson
to be memorized;
ours must be Understood.

Let the thin, bloodless men
who are the educated sons
of ribbon clerks
spin the broken-glass facts
of Vietnam into a golden yarn
to be woven, years later,
into the rich, cultural tapestry
of world history.
It will be of little meaning
and less consequence;
a history of dates and times
and petty accuracies of who-hit-Johns.

Fact is only a portion of any truth
and the academic disciplines of today
view life through a narrow window
(screening out both lux et veritas)
And rationale is not enough to live on.

Color is to the eye
what perspective is to the mind;
it lends balance.
But not all the red and blue arrows
sweeping from all the pages
of the Vietnam history books
will give any hint of human direction
beyond the deployment
of allied and enemy troops.
There will be no explanation
of any part of the real war;
the inner war.
The actions and passions of life
are not confronted
nose to nose
by historians.
Therefore, they do not FEEL IT.
(And are loath in their accounts
to moralize it).
They TEACH the history
that men such as you have LIVED
and that fallen comrades
such as we have loved
have DIED . . .
No one should write bloodlessly
of spilled blood.

Certainly, the only valid text
that will ever be written
about the Vietnam War
has already been written:
The Book of Names.

Somewhere, this Memorial Day
some of us will read it aloud
from cover to cover.
And it will be too big to comprehend.
It is doomed like the men it represents
to be a part of the outer war
unless we take it "inside."
If we are ever to explain
the true cost of the war,
better by far
to pick one name
and read aloud
from his last love letter . . .

From coast to coast
we seem to be arranging
an almost instinctive,
undeniable pattern
of Vietnam veterans
An enormous, living,
connect-the-dots puzzle
that will spell out
the ultimate truth of Vietnam
(from the sequential understanding
of our combined inner wars).

As with all pointilism
the individual dot seems lost
and unimportant.
Alone, we appear without validity.
Our separate inner truths
did not translate into English
(or Vietnamese)
its language voiced itself
in isolated rage;
often incomprehensible
(even to ourselves)
and always inappropriate.
Yet, together we seem
clearly to be outlining
an unmistakably Reasonable statement
large enough for all the world to see
in its completed form:
NO MORE WAR.
It is almost as if we were part
of some imponderable design
an intricate and inexplicable
as winter snowflakes must be
to a migrating duck.

It is time for our truth.
It feels right.
The classical Greeks knew it all along.
(The nature of man is best known
by considering nature itself).
It took Ulysses twenty years
to return from the wars

and put his house in order.
It's taken twenty years
to get from the Gulf of Tonkin Incident
to here and now.
And it's taken twenty years
for this country to raise its children
to be the average age
of the college student to whom
the subject of Vietnam is addressed
and to whom the next war
seems ready to be served.

Therefore, let you and I
continue to join
with our brothers and sisters
and speak today
(and every day)
for truth and humanity
(while there is still time).
And if any should ask, Why Us?
We shall give them this good reason:
We went to Vietnam
as American fighting men
and came back
as human beings
(that's why we didn't feel
at home right away).
And until we found each other
we didn't understand our responsibility
to that kind of citizenship.
And now that we do,
WE HAVE IT TO DO!

Ever, there are things by which men
seem willing to live
and things, therefore, for which they
seem willing to die.
As for me (if I have a choice)
rather than lead one million boys to war
I would prefer to die alone for peace.

Such is the history lesson
of my inner war.
It may not be yours.
Our task is not to agree—
it is simply to add our truth
to the sum of all truth.

In that will be a legacy
worthy of our sacrifice
and a monument
fit to mark
the end of our war . . .

ANGRY LITTLE POEM OF SPRING

This poem speaks of the keen sense of justice and appropriate moral outrage which have become characteristic of the Vietnam veteran.

ANGRY LITTLE POEM
OF SPRING

During the off-season
my libido sits in the crisper
with the lettuce
and food becomes the only love
I can accept,
but with the coming of spring
the celebration of my life
begins anew in an instinctive,
ring-around-the-rosies party
to which my blood invites only itself;
a pep rally of my ancestors—
and never, never does my reason
seek attendance . . .

The little genetic smurfs
(spelunking deep within me)
sing a Hi! Ho! gonadian marching song
the lyrics for which
will never be published,
but hum along quite nicely
about long legs and longer nights
(light on the violins, please—
Heavy on the drums)

zing zing zing I love you
BOOM BOOM BOOM!!! That's it.
By God, I think you've got it!
Why in over a quarter of a century
I have not so much as Seen
an ugly woman in April!
(They have either taken to hiding
or are invisible to my passion.)

Each year,
on the eve of the vernal equinox,
I am so physically pumped
and psychically stumped
(I don't know nothin' 'bout nothin'
and jez wanna do it ALL)
I stand in the open door
of my refrigerator
waiting for my libido to thaw.
And not being interested
in the chocolate covered Grahams
for the first time in six months,
I take a slow count of ten
and feel the collective knowledge
of fourteen hundred generations
of mankind (to have my eyes)
course through my veins
like one thousand, four hundred gondolas
steered by the separate, romantic
(sometimes desperate) adventures
of all my Italian grandfathers
negotiating 35,000 years

of my modern-man's blood
like Venetian sailors in the blind;
each ferrying a precious lesson-learned
like it was a reclining Cleopatra
on the prow.
One at a time, they dock at the pier of my brain
faster than you
canflickthepagesofHGWELLSOutlineofHistory
to drop off their annual springtime
Hail-to-the-last-of-the-line advice
on all the major issues;
Sex, war, rock & roll, Dante Alighieri
and pasta al dente.
And boy, do I listen to these consiglioris
of my loins!
Hell, first grandsire to "tie-up"
to my reason each spring,
kicked Neanderthal ass
right out of Europe.
But confidentially speaking, of course,
there IS Something There
(if you get my meaning)
about a short, squat Neanderthal MaMa
whose ass I sense he DIDN'T kick one spring
(who looked like a Neapolitan gorilla
wearing Bella Abzug's hat)
which probably accounts for my wearing one
even indoors at the typewriter—
if you think Levi's wear forever,
you should try outrunning
your Real genes!

This year his offering to me was
that ugly women aren't invisible
it's just that love is blind!
(Old guy thinks it's original—
which for him it really is—
so each year I laugh like hell.
He likes that.)

I got one grandfather was born
four years, two days before
the Bronze Age;
Worked out a seven-page solution
to the question of his Age
(how to compute the area of a triangle)
actually, he scratched his formula
on a hundred-yard strip of beach
not far from Nice at low tide
and never got credit for his work.
Six hours later he forgot the whole thing,
but I know he did it.
In 1951 I was taught the formula
was simply ½bh—knowing that was pure
Bullshit, I purposely flunked math
for the rest of my life. Out of respect.
I suspect Grandfather was a purist
who liked to be careful
(that's how come we got this far)
none of those guys did sloppy work;
we're the proof of that.
Each year I feel him give me
the same advice—Go slow . . .

Oh yes, how sweet it is
to be eternally moored
on the universal questions
of your generation;
of your life—
Shoot, my reason is only in its early forties,
but my instinct is as old as God.
You think I'm gonna preempt how I FEEL
with what I THINK? Hell, no . . .
my reason sits on my instinct like a chimpanzee
on the back of a runaway mastodon.

Take, for instance, the kids.
Ever wonder why all they do is play?
Because it's their job.
And it may be the most serious one
they'll ever get.

All young practice at play
the skills they will need later
to survive as adults;
two kittens with a ball of yarn,
three boys in a tree,
me and Lydia in the garage
(I was always afraid of heights).

With repetition each skill
becomes second nature
(actually it's first nature,
but we don't know how to say that).
After several hundred generations
nobody has to practice very long
to get a thing down pat.
Like when somebody hollers,
HEADS UP! everybody pulls his head DOWN!
But nature doesn't trust us
with the truly important things.
Like how to convert
the gaseous metabolism of an onion
into a life-saving burp.
Or how to hold a baby in your arms
so it can find comfort
in the rhythm of your heartbeat.
Some things we are just "born knowing."

Sometimes kids (and whole species)
stay at the same game too long
and get hurt
or wander off to play
in the wrong neighborhood
and are never heard from again.

I'll tell you brothers and sisters,
this ROCK-TOSS, BALL-THROW,
GRENADE-PITCH, BOMB-DROP, LASER-BEAM,
out-of-this-world, hostile spiral
we are on is going way past dark
and I think I hear Mother Nature
calling each of us by name—
And we're in the WRONG PART OF TOWN,
now . . .

Certainly, there is no such thing
as a flat roller-coaster
or a FUN House without HORROR
(life is so terrifying,
even our play must be thrilling)
But our concept of fun has always been
the back-alley play of violence and risk
and because we have evolved to this
Time & Place on the strengths developed
from action and passion
we believe we are irrevocably committed
to that tree-top mentality. We are wrong.

The sheet-draped wings of the stodgy museums
are filled with frantic, little wimps
making plaster-of-Paris reconstructions
of whole species and other chump societies
which failed to modify their behavior
(in time) . . .
It's almost paralyzing to me
that probably 99% of all the species
which ever were, are no more
and 95% of all the scientists
who ever lived, are still alive!
What, therefore, are our chances?

The alternative to nonviolence
is not nonexistence; it is Peace.
And we must begin to Practice Practice.
Is there, anywhere in the world, a mother
screaming from her front door
(in any language)
"Johnny, for the LAST time—
PUT DOWN those peace treaties
and come in the house this INSTANT—
you can play GENEVA CONVENTION
after Dinner!" . . . ?

Shit.
No wonder there are over a hundred
shooting wars going on in the world.

Well, after Vietnam it was as if you and I
were just "born knowing"
that if we don't want our grandchildren
to grow up breathing ammonia through a straw,
waiting for a corporal or a carpenter
to show them a way out,
WE'RE going to have to point the way, NOW!
We are as responsible to our evolutionary past
as we are to our visionary future.
We must begin to accept the reality
of what CAN BE
with the equal certainty
of what HAS BEEN.
WE'VE GOT IT TO DO!!!

You know, man is the only animal
who can look both ways;
can you imagine
stepping into a time corridor,
craning your neck down the hall
to see the long, backward line
of all your ancestors
going back, say as far
as Homo Erectus
and calling them to attention?
"Excuse me. Excuse me, please!
Can you hold it down just a bit,
I have a short administrative
announcement to make . . . Ahem,
thank you, ah, you remember the Ice Age?
And the ah, earthquakes and the time

Great Grandfather to the 4th power
back there stepped in whale shit
and almost drowned, but dragged home
the leaves anyway? (The magic ones
that stopped Grandma's bleeding.)
And you remember (just like it was
yesterday) when Guiseppe-the-bum
got the Black Death and just before
he died, stole the butcher's purse
and gave it to his son standing
in front of him here, Lorenzo?
Raise your hand Lorenzo—come on
for chrissake raise your hand—
ALL Right! Thank you Grandpa.
And what did he tell you
when he gave you the purse—
Remember? Yeah, me too. Just like
it was yesterday. And it's OK
to cry, we're all family here, right?
Sure, he said, 'Lorenzo, stay in school.'
Good words. Yeah, well, I just
want all of you to know
that for the past 1.2 million years
it's been, well, a helluva ride.
But it's over . . .''
And can you imagine stepping back inside
picking up your own child
and waiting for the bomb to drop???
CAN YOU IMAGINE THAT???
IT'S WHAT THE WORLD IS DOING!!!

Well, our combined genetic intelligence
can no longer be externalized
in the primitive, attack-muscled mind set
which builds munitions factories
while babies starve.
We are in the Information Age now.
(Well, maybe not a few former marines
I know, but most of us anyway.)
We are in an age where nimble wit
and negotiations are the only
acceptable tools
for resolving the differences
of a burgeoning world population
expected (with God's help)
to reach 6 billion souls
by the turn of the century.

Systems must be managed,
but people must be led.
Where are our LEADERS?
Men of moral courage
of music of values
of vision and dreams?
Everywhere I look,
from government building
to government building,
I see merchants. Businessmen.
Who are these fucking accountants
who manage our destinies
as if mankind were the private stock room
of the trilateral commission

and the pentagonal shoe clerks?
Who are they to share the hegemony
of the Third World as if
there really was more than one?
Who are these old men
who look at the world map
as if they were considering a merger
of K-mart and Sears
and see the young men of the world
sweeping their floors gratefully?

Life is not a business
and cannot be run for profit.
We (you and I)
have brothers in jail
whose sons are hungry—
our government embraces dictators
and sends them millions and millions
(later they will send the sons)
God, if they pass the prayer amendment,
what should the kids pray for?
Food? or Favorable winds?
Damn.

Yes. I am angry.
You would be too
if you had YOUR HEAD
stuck in the fridge
since the first day of spring . . .

The counsel of my grandfathers
was ending and I was just about
to fill my mouth to bursting
with pale, green grapes
take one enormous FROSH! FRIP!!
and squish myself to sweet madness
or choke to death on delicious giggles,
when I heard on the radio
that the aircraft carrier Kittyhawk
had just collided
with a Soviet, Viktor-class submarine!
What the fuck? over.
I mean, what IS THAT?
The world is getting ready
to replenish itself
and two, would-be admirals
are simulating a technological,
mating dance in the Sea of Japan.
It's the one they choreographed
for opus Armageddon
(in c-sharp for lute, metal and water)
that's the one with the really great chorus
at the end (when the sea gives up its dead)
and the rest of the world goes
down
the
drain . . .

But that's not what made me mad.
It was the pentagon applauding,
GOOD SHOW! that pissed me off.
That. And one thing more . . .
On that very same day in Soho
(Greenwich Village)
a Japanese girl danced naked
in the streets
to celebrate the renewal of life—
a smiling crowd of human beings
was told it was against the law.

Oh, I see.
Actually I didn't see until Grandpa Vito
pulled me back into the fridge
and told me to cool it
with a nudge from the groin.
I could feel him tell me,
"Boy, crime don't pay on a small scale,
it pays on a Big one.
And if that crime becomes big enough
it begins to govern—
and boy, the only way to protect yourself
from a thing that don't love you,
is to surround yourself with family who do."

"Yes, Grandpa," I said aloud, "I'll remember.
I know who my brothers and sisters are
and from now on
we'll take good care
of each other."

I promise.

70

THE CASUALTY

This poem was written as a definition of war and as a description of the men who fought in Vietnam. It is a statement of courage and continued commitment.

THE CASUALTY

I.

In the final end
we will have loved
more dreams than people;
given Time, some dreams come true—
most people prove false.
Truth, it seems, is an agreement
not long kept by friends and lovers;
it functions best between enemies
for whom the illusion of truth
is spirit for the first deceit.

These days,
like you, I am an expert in disbelief.
War in Vietnam and Peace in America
have imbued in us a God-like detachment;
a perceptual handicap,
which interdicts most lies.
For us,
neither the president,
nor the emperor,
wears clothes.

And it remains the truest illusion of our war
that it is over;
the grandest delusion of our peace
that is begun . . .

It begins with simply this:
that each man goes to his war
as he goes to his love; alone.
And from neither does he return as before.
For love and war exist
at the edges of the human experience
and whether new-born or quick-dead,
life hangs in the balance.
Either way, man grapples with his universe
at the very limits of social restraint.
His cultural upbringing
too weak to govern
in the province of the darkness
and the dawn.

To survive in combat
a man must turn
from the teachings of other men
and come face to face with himself;
mano a mano.
In the dark,
instinct is a more perfect mirror
than reason.
And its first image
hurls the stone
which shatters the greatest lie

of his life;
that he is not alone.
For some it is a joy
to come to know such a man as he is.
For others, it is a nightmare
which recurs so long as he may live.

The world of the combat soldier
is a flat one
whose highest peak is mean survival
and whose lowest value
is the killing of his enemy.
It is a private world
of height without depth
from which can be viewed
the separate, fractured worlds
of comrades dying
(as from a galactic distance).
Strange, how close is a dead buddy;
how far is recalling his laughter.

It is a world
of unaccountable and indefinite season
where time is measured
by the Xing of the days
like the labored wall-scratchings
of condemned men.

It is a stereophonic world
of unspecified dimension
bordered on all sides by fear
and weathered by the tiny cloud puffs
of hope and prayer and dream
and a letter from home
which does not speak
of bills
or broken bones
or the unspeakable Death
of faithfulness.

War is a surrealistic penal colony
for young patriots of the real world
who, as sons of poor men,
must pay the price
for the believable myths
of national furors and private enterprise.

War as a social statement
has the depth of a slit trench at Argonne.
And echoes about as long
as it took the blood to dry at Hue.

When he wrestles at the edge
of his private, first-class world
where his least backward step
will plummet him into the cosmic promise
of his belief system,
each man knows
that in this, his final battle,

he fights neither for glory nor justice,
not for wealth
nor a cushioned seat
in the Kingdom of Heaven.
Not for country. Not for freedom.
He fights for the approval of his loved ones.
And he fights for his life.

If honor is to light the way to his Maker
it burns most brightly
when he sacrifices his life
for another.
In that gesture, humanity survives war.
And Peace clings
by a desperate finger
to a belt loop
of the stern, and long-striding History
of mankind
marching inexorably
toward some never-to-be-printed,
final date.

The combat veteran of Vietnam
lived in a world
where medals occasionally pinned themselves
on donkeys
and the green disappeared from the trees—
attacked by the one word in his language
which refused to rhyme;
Orange.

Years later,
it would bleach the rainbows
from his children's eyes
and then, nothing rhymed.
(not even God)
and least of all, DOW.

The combat trooper searched to destroy.
In the end,
as a veteran,
he searched only to understand.
In Vietnam he looked for a reason.
And found none.
At home he looked for approval.
and found none.
From the million, separate ledges
of his lonely worlds,
he jumped.
One
at
a
time
like lemmings into the sea.

Today,
many Vietnam vets
still hang
suspended
under
the floating shelves of their former worlds—
each by a single strand of sanity

more narrow than a window-washer's rope,
oscillating slowly into middle-age
as from a madman's drool.
His family watches
from a window
ten stories
higher than the moon
unable to reach him
unable to understand him
unable to be unable
anymore.

The veteran swings between
murder   and   suicide.
His journey is the plain geometry
of conscience;
a pendulum's arc
tracing across the face of the sky
a child's smile
which asks the unspoken question,
"Who speaks for the little ones?"

II.

When a spider climbs her single thread
into the eaves of the roof
she does so to live the good life
unnoticed.

The rope-climbing Nam vet
who pulls for the safety of main street,
trusts to his proven techniques
of cover and concealment
to protect him.
He does so with no thought
to the good life;
rather as a final,
instinctive pull and lunge
for survival.

For those who make it
to the top of the world
only to enter the closet,
fear is the fifth wall
in an ever-closing room.
Death by emotional starvation awaits.
So much for cover.

From the mangrove swamps
to the suburban closets,
the Vietnam vet survives
in the emotional tenements of his world.
But the city cousin
who wears his bush hat
to camouflage the truth
of who and what he is
(better even than in the jungle)
survives barely at all—
and brings unwanted attention
(of the wrong kind)

to the rest of us.
For in the swamps,
our camouflage offered protective coloration;
we blended with it all (in a quiet oneness).
But in the asphalt jungle
our camouflage stands out
as WARNING coloration.
Instinctively, the frightened vet
seeks to protect himself
by raising "Jolly-Roger"
and chasing the citizens away.

In nature, a species warning others
of his danger
is favorably rewarded.
In civilization (within the same group)
the warning
is a hostile statement
generating fear, anger, avoidance
and ultimately, retaliation.
Jungle fatigues are not varsity sweaters.
And if pride and group-recognition
should be our motive,
then understatement should be our wardrobe.
If the wimps of the world
wear alligators on their shirts
can't we wear jungle boots on ours?

Time enough to figure how to live
when all of us are back on top.
But how to get us all back up?
So many of us
at
the
end
of
our
ropes . . .

Well, remember those yuk-yuk,
backslapping, Brylcreem days
of the gridiron club meetings?
(What world was that?)
Those dreamy, green-tinted afternoons
when the giggles
of the future wives of America
floated through our windows
as they practiced the cheers
which would send us against
our dreaded, hated enemies next Saturday.
And the Saturday after that.
Bringing our enemies with it.
Strange, nobody seemed to notice
how after the first kickoff
the ambulance
would quietly pull behind the bleachers
(maybe it was bad luck to mention it).
God were we set up!

Women, cheers, uniforms, decorations,
parades, proud parents AND
the National Anthem!
What a life! When we were seventeen.

When we were eighteen
in Vietnam
only the ambulance showed up.
And when we got back home
somebody'd moved the town . . .

Well, maybe it didn't work.
But still it was a good dream.
A good way of life.
And so, we need another dream, that's all.
Hell, the one thing all suicides
have in common
is that each has lost his sense of humor.
C'mon bro, would you really
rather have been upstairs
in that airless room
(with the closed transom)
discussing the amount of sodium
on the back of a 2¢ King Louis
with the nerds of the stamp club?
Or been with us—fast and loose—
at street level
where the rubber meets the road?
At gut level, where a man meets a man?
Shit. C'mon bro, it's me you're talkin' to.
Shit.

Didn't lose any wars WE were in.
Didn't break any dreams WE believed.
Snap out of it, bro! Hear me!
We didn't lose anybody's fuckin' war.
We kicked ass!
We didn't break anybody's mutha fuckin' dream.
WE BOUGHT IT!!
Shit.
It was THEM.
THEY pulled out on US.
The moral equivalent of desertion
under fire.
The country didn't confuse the warrior
with the war.
They knew who we were.
It's themselves they loathe
and tried to avoid.
We merely remind them
of who they really are—
of their lack of courage:
moral and physical.
It takes strength to believe
and balls to put it on the line—
we had both.
They had neither.
And there's no such thing as benign envy.

But you know what?
After all the stories are told
and all the seas are salt,
it was you and me, bro,
who caught the fish;
who cut the fish.
We, the men;
ours, the dream.
Because we were together, we were strong.
And can be again!

We pulled ourselves out of the jungle mud
one buddy at a time.
And we can pull ourselves
out of this shit, too.
(if we pull for each other)

You know,
I'll bet if the families of our brothers
killed-in-action
could sign a petition
charging each combat veteran of Vietnam
to live his life
as if he were living for two,
half of us would be on top of the world
by tomorrow afternoon!

A man may fight for his life
on a personal level,
but when he loves,
he does so for all mankind.

When we had no other reason to fight
in Vietnam
we fought for each other.
Today, in America,
it's still a good reason
to keep fighting.
Where once we saved each other
from death,
now we have the chance to save each other
for life!

Hey! bro,
when we're over the top?
whadya say?
We fix the place up a little
for the kids, ya know?
Tell 'em a dream
they can make come true
An' then jez hunker down
to watch 'em grow.

. . . and let no grim, graybeard of a god
speak again to us of glory
by bodycount.

CLOSURE:
A MUCH NEEDED WAR

This epilogue of the National Salute II addresses in part each veteran's continuing commitment to citizenship; as an American and as a human being. It was shared in New York City on May 7, 1985, on the Aircraft Carrier Intrepid as part of the official activities following the parade down Fifth Avenue and the dedication of the New York Vietnam Veterans Memorial.

CLOSURE:
A MUCH NEEDED WAR

I.

It had been a long war there.
It had been a long war back.
Neither way had been easy.
But still, the ultimate victory
of the Vietnam War
was never to be military.
And it was Always to be ours.
So we came this Veterans Day
to the nation's capital.
We came by the thousands.
We came by the tens of thousands.
We came by the hundreds of thousands.
And we came alone.
Each to make his peace with America.
For each man knew in his own way
that whether he was physically detained
by the enemy
or spiritually captured
by his own conscience,

a prisoner of war
could only be repatriated
by the efforts of his government.
So come we did.
And the unity we found
is being sung
in the clear, and unmistakable voice
of an entire generation.

It was the measure of us
that predicted it—
that hallmark willingness to commit,
that trademark reluctance to quit—
on all sides of the conflict.
Do you remember who we were?
Those of us who went to war
had to be dragged out;
Those of us who stayed at home
(to fight against that war)
had to be dragged away.
We are all veterans
of the Vietnam War.

And our victory was won
in the character of our sacrifice
and the quality of our loss.

Yet, despite the fact that we came
to nationalize "Our Wall,"
there is a haunting feeling
of irresolution.
Of no closure. Why?
We got what we came for, didn't we?
We came to throw down
our field jackets, right?
To take some tracings of the "names"
and maybe (while nobody was lookin')
to drop off a little something
near your buddy's name
that would've made him laugh
(I left a beer cap
from a bottle of "33"
and tried to fake a burp
like Johnny always did).
Shit. They don't print directions
on the backsides of walls do they?
A man's gotta play it "by heart."

To tell you the truth,
I heard a lotta guys talkin'
and I could see from your faces
some of you were bein' answered.
It's all about love and loss, isn't it?

But what about closure?
The government promised to take care
of The Wall
(probably water it twice a day).
The nurses are sure to get a statue
in the next couple of years.
We heard a candlelit, Navy Admiral
tell us the POW/MIA issue
was the "nation's highest priority"
(I quietly put out my candle
and walked).
The president spoke.
Closure.
End of story.
Exuent stage left.
Pass the baton. Whatever turns you off.
It's over . . .
Does it feel over to you?
Me neither.
Shit.

II.

Maybe we should back it up a bit . . .

Nobody ever
wanted to belong
like we did.
To belong to a thing so beautiful.
So right. So alive.
One, sweet breath after another,
being an American
was a lot like breathing.
How could you not?

Well, after Vietnam
many of us did try to hold our breath.
Fists jammed deep into our pockets,
we turned our collars up
and walked through marriages and jobs,
nightmares and daymares
clear across America.
Eyes on the curb of our sanity
we whistled the red, white and blues
like we were blown
through James Moody's flute
till there was no air left
(even to cry the blues).

As for me,
I darted across my reality
like somebody let loose
the pinched ends
of a too full balloon.
Whizzzzzzz!
And I bounced off the wall

useless and spent
into a leather crack
at the front edge of a donated Vet Center chair
(right next to you)
looking like I felt—
a limp dick.
(And as I recall, hah!
you didn't look so fuckin' great
yourself.)

So we sat there
(all across the country)
in small, unmerry little bands
looking, no doubt, from each ceiling
like a large, nervous smoke ring!
And proceeded to huff and puff
and talk our way
out of the jungle,
all the way home.
One day, each of our group leaders
will be bronzed
and appropriately awarded,
unto himself, a park.
Until then,
they'll have to be content
with merely having saved
a lot of lives.
My team leader was Bill Mahedy.
I would have been history
five years ago . . .

Oh, those group sessions!
  "Yeah, and my specialty
  was cuttin' ears off . . ."

  "Shit. I been married to more women
  than is in this room right now.
  I mean than there is guys
  in this room right now. Oh shit.
  You know what I mean . . ."

  "I don't trust anybody. Not anybody.
  Not even my kids. Not even the dog."

  "I'll give those muthas the benefit
  of my education. I'll go ninja
  and blow up every V.A. building
  in the country!"
  (Many cheers and catcalls
  and a chorus of Fuckin A's!!!)
An' my group had a dumbass in it!
who would say things like,
  "Man is probably the only animal
  who takes prisoners.
  Certainly, he is the only one
  who denies whole portions
  of his population access
  to the general food supply . . ."
Boy, was I a dumbass
but everybody was nice to me
(I brought the doughnuts).
I maintained I had existential anxiety,

they maintained I was just a dumbass.
God, what perspective!
I loved those guys.
And I like to think
they loved me back.

When the group would break up
we'd take it outside to the fenders.
Sometimes until dawn.
The night air helped cool the rage.
We discussed how to make a difference.
At such times I could feel America
listening to our conversations
as she lay in bed. Thinking.

Well. America woke up.
And she continued to listen.
And finally she sat down
across the table from us
and she just called our hand.
I figure we're holding
aces over jacks—
truth over courage.
And if she agrees—
we've won the pot
and the deal.
And the deal is:
We're out of the box now.
Out of the closet.
We're standin' in the door
and "outside" we've got it to do.
Only our war is over.

America is waiting for us, now.
And the world is waiting for America.
It won't be enough to wear buttons.
It won't be enough to coach
a girls' softball team
when the children of other poor men
are too weak to stand.
It's our play now.
The truth of our perspective
must be assimilated
by our nation's system of values.
And added to the consciousness
of the world.
Until then, no closure.

III.

I believe somewhere, everywhere
there is the generic veteran
for whom no national border,
nor ethnic pride
is grand enough
to color his humanity.
I believe also,
that it is this world's
most brave champions
who dream of peace
and each country's truest sons
who must live for it.
And, therefore,
not this Veterans Day

nor the next
nor the one after that
will men and women of my heart
find closure for the war we fought
in a ceremony honoring the dead.
(We cherish them best who gave it all
by dedicating our lives to the living.)
For closure, if such exists,
comes only to the warrior.
The veteran, is of other matter.
Truth under fire
has tempered each veteran
of Every war
from one part warrior
and one part human being.
And for each of Us
(long before closure)
there remains one, much needed war.
One, last commitment
worthy of a lifetime—
to fight for peace
in each of our hearts
against the fierce enemies
of our darkest natures.
And to march in lock-step
with veterans of all wars
from all nations
for human dignity.

Then shall we pass in review
and each will hear
mankind whisper to the gods,
"There then, goes one of ours."

SPECIAL POEMS

Untitled poem delivered at St. Paul's Church, San Diego, California on December 18, 1981, as part of a national prayer-in for the first delegation of Vietnam Veterans to return to Vietnam. Original poem presently hangs in war museum, Hanoi, Republic of Vietnam.

Somewhere,
High in the attic
   of our collective conscience
in a special, closed-off corner of our minds
      more dark than our fears
      more real than our dreams
is a door
behind which is locked Our war (Vietnam)
   a large, salivating dog; faithless & mad
snarling in the muffled upward reaches
                                    of our reason—
Howling against the thin, rare echo
                        of our long stale youth—
Scratching and clawing—hurling itself
   against the ever-weakening barrier of our sanity;
Our entire house trembles
at its presence
As We,
Two floors
   pointless years

and twelve thousand miles below
huddle our heads
in mute prayer
   in the living-rooms of our (once) normal lives—
For tonight, in that stale garret
of our timeless souls
just outside the monstrous obscenity
                              of our unresolved guilt
            and speechless rage
                              at senseless death

Near the ladder
pulled up from the floor below
Sit Four Americans,
Four Human Beings
Four of Us
Representing Each of us;
There, in a circle of personal conviction
                              reverent in intensity
                              irreverent in willfulness
amidst the rubble of our scattered youth
strewn like discarded Christmas wrappings
               on the cracked and splintered planks,
they doodle with the incessant fingers
                         of our shame and sadness
         in the sawdust droppings
                   of our irrefutable, remnant humanity
         the scrawled names
of our captured
and fallen friends
still locked behind
That dreaded door.

And (perhaps) at this precise moment
in Time & Space they raise aloft
    a single candle
            of hope
against the now silent entrance
        to reach with a strength and a sacrifice
    known best to the families
of those brave men who wait below
behind clenched teeth
and only (for the sake of the children)
pretend to breathe.
And now they raise their common voice
and call out for all the world of men to hear,
                "We are only men here
                Who is in there with you?
                Alive or Dead
                The Truth will out;
                In the Name of Mankind
                Let them Free
                or forever be known
                for What you Are . . ."

None of us here tonight
can anticipate the response—if any
Yet, each of us knows
No mad dog exists (nor ever did)
that at the first light
of the candle
the madness and uncontrolled rage
will diminish into stern truth only
& the muffled growlings will be heard

as sterner questions
requiring still sterner answers—
And yet, how understandable
How stupidly Human
that we did not at first consider
that This house
layered floor upon
floor,
filled with each of our lives
and leading to that grim
                         and frightful attic
is a duplex;
joined at the very hinges of the earth
                         half a world away
filled with the Southeast Asian farmers
represented in the attic
by Four Vietnamese
who sit in common conscience
and reach with universal courage
and Mandarin grace
for a doorknob
behind which seems to growl
a mad dog
not knowing
what they will find—
or maybe,
there is no such thing as coincidence.
Maybe as God rewinds
                         His celestial watch
slipping the gears of Time & Space
                         to realign the window of our world,

we will notice that tonight
the Little hand points to Christmas
and the Big hand reads seven days

                            before the Hour—
and Maybe, it *is* the Right time
                to move to that window of our hopes
and wait prayerfully for the star in the East
to Rise Again
on a new and real dawning of peace.

                    humbly offered by
                    Steve Mason
                    former Captain, US Army
                    combat veteran, Vietnam

Delivered at the Shoreham Hotel, Washington, D.C., November 7, 1983, for the First National Convention of the Vietnam Veterans of America. Reprinted here exactly as it was scribbled on the hotel placemats.

FOUNDING CONVENTION POEM

I have looked death in the eye
and spat blood
I have faced life squarely
and made love
I am a combat veteran
of Vietnam
And not altogether certain
of my direction,
But sure of myself—
A delegate enroute
to a national convention
And proud to count for more
than my pain;

At 30,000 feet there are
no flat clouds
Which point to the nation's
capital
No calendars to enumerate
a just-right world
Of sequential firmness
on-going below,
My unresolved hurt
makes it difficult
to look out this small
round window
And know beyond reason
what time & place
my mind suspends
outboard this aircraft—
I look to see
a mirrored on-board image
of myself
& question with a hard blink
& a sharp eye,
Where are my epaulettes?
Who took the hash marks
from my sleeve?
Damn—It's been a long time
between rides
A long time since I looked out
another aircraft window
& watched real life
Refracted across
the lawns of the world—

Sat helpless as the thick,
plastic window
distorted the courage
of my innocence
So that I might
distinguish capitalist jungles
from communist jungles
at a distance of 6 miles
straight up . . .

I was a soldier/statesman
on that flight also
Gone to represent my government
in Vietnam
& today I fly to Washington
to represent 35 former statesmen
from that earlier flight
Funny flights
Funny world—
And time won't make
sense of it
But you and I will try . . .

And I stare unfocused
thru the blur
of bending light
& passing time
& use this porthole-like window
as a rewind button
To blink those just-postwar years back
& know the pain

from which my courage comes
And I begin to feel
the reality of war
debunk the illusion
of my upbringing
And I sense that I have quickly become
the shadow man I was—
Detached, alone—
drowning in myself
Stranded like a pubic hair
in an airport urinal—
Those just-postwar years
when suicide was sad companion
to my nights
& sat at my bedside
writing notes with me
till dawn
& never left a single one—
for at dawn's early light
As if it had been sprung
From the promise of my wallpaper
in a long gone childhood dream
I would be rescued
By my cowboy, cut n' shoot
John Wayne rage—Ha Hah!
Yeh, if it was woeful suicide
that got me thru my nights
it was heroic rage
that swept me thru my days.

You know the kind.
I thank God
you and I
are men of passion

& I know that even
the poorest of records
of this madder
than mad world
will show that
Whether suicide or homicide
generally only one life
hangs in the balance,

But indifference manufactures
death on a planetary scale
and calls it something grand
occasionally putting it to music

Maybe that's why
there is no wallpaper
anywhere in the world
for an eight-year-old boy
with pictures of thin, bloodless
technocrats
waving briefcases
at passing taxicabs—
Maybe that's why there's cowboys
on the walls of America

But whether suicide or
homicide or genocide
one day we are all asked
to choose a "cide"

As this convention will ask
my conscience
which side it is on
(on other more brave issues)
And I hope whatever my answer
it will echo in agreement with the voices
of a thousand, thousand veterans

Ah, we can make it happen
you & I
we've still got it to do . . .

The plane pitched slightly
an errant right elbow
struck me from reverie
The onboard movie was
a romantic comedy,
But the man with
the too pink face
next to me
was pornographic—
Nobody seemed to notice, but
me as he masturbated
his pocket computer
with a fantastic combination
of obscene numbers:

2 of these
& one of those
3 of these & not a single one of the others
combinations with bottom line results
not concerned with
the human condition
An occasional ecstatic sigh
escaped from his credit card smile

I leaned away from him
Back into my chair

And looking out the window
pushed the fast forward
to consider my own numbers

How 'bout U.S. rangers
jumping onto the airstrip
at 500 feet!

Do you have any idea
what that number marks, sucker?

I hit the rewind again
for a split second
& stopped at 229

Hey, you want numbers
I got numbers
Howse 229 killed
young guys in Lebanon
who found out that death
is the only dream
from which you can't wake screaming

Put that in your wafer-thin
designer computer
Mr. tecnocraft

& I'll talk to you, of tetrytol
& primacord
of lost legs
and long gone grunts

You know something
you sonovabitch
you don't look familiar to me—
Where were you
when we were in Vietnam?
Funny, how many guys
"were ready to go"
whose numbers just
didn't come up
in the lottery

Funnier, most of the guys I knew
weren't ready to go—but went anyway

And then the heavy numbers
jumped at the windows
grabbed at the wings
& shook the plane
Like a cyclone
with the force
of their meaning:
57,000 KIA
248,000 WIA
& then the nausea
which had nothing to do
with air sickness came

As the whispered whimperings
of my reptilian mind
clawed at the cortex
of my reason
"How many of us
did you leave behind?"

My balls turned to jelly
and the guy next to me
belched on his scotch.

You want higher math,
Computer-man?
If we left only one MIA/POW
behind—that number & its loss
are incalculable.

Thank goodness
the stewardess
told me to straighten-up
for landing
And I thanked her
for her attendance
& especially
for "the real whole milk"
she smiled blankly
I offered lamely
It was an inside joke, you see,
Knowing somewhere
there was an entire generation
of 40-year-old stews
who knew what
"real whole milk"
was all about
(and I want to make love
to all of 'em)

And the wheels
rumbled down
As I prepared
to hit the ground running
Shuffling to the exit door
I reminded myself to
vote as a representative
not as an individual
And that conscience
without balls
becomes guilt

Just as government
without philosophy
becomes only power

The door opened slow & wide
on the day of the Vietnam veterans—blue & sweet
For men who have ratified
the constitution of this nation
with sweat & blood
And will now help
formulate its philosophy
with pride & truth.
Feeling profound respect
for all our fallen comrades
to the standing ovation
of our now grateful children . . .

This poem was delivered as the keynote address in Spokane, Washington, on November 10, 1985, at the unveiling of the Inland Northwest Vietnam Veterans Memorial. United States Government dignitaries were in attendance with political leadership from the states of Washington, Idaho, and Montana.

THE CHILDREN OF THE SUN

I.

My brothers and my sisters,
I will be remembered one day
not for anything I say
nor for anything I do,
but because I was with you
one day when it mattered
and we stood together in the sun.

And you of my heart must know
that if I should grant myself a dream
let it be that when it is over
I could live my life again with you,
that we might share a better world
on a day made brighter by our truth . . .

We are met at Riverfront Park
beneath the watchful and timely face
of the Old Railroad Clock.
It is that monument to the movement and record
of this locale which reminds us of our place
in this land which is ours
on this world of which we are a part.

How many fond hellos
still echo in its chimes?
How many brave goodbyes
still tremble in the ear
of this community?

We stand in our place today
on the surface
of a land much loved
and deeply layered
in the sediment of all life
and in the human tradition
to value and respect
the bringer of that life.

This bountiful land has been a crossroads
for creatures great and small
who loved it well.
And those of you who were born here
know well the stories
of the time before the Clock . . .

They called them Spokan-ee
"The Children of the Sun,"
those brave and gentle grandsons
of the "Old Ones who went before."
They walked and rode
the Cascades to the Rockies
from far to the south
to far into the north
those proud and peaceful citizens
of the great Inland Northwest.
And all their trails
of hunting and of dreams
met here
at Spokan Falls.

What they set out to do
and where they are today
is all that we will ever come to know
of wind and mist
and shooting stars
of ponies' hooves in sand.
They are as April in the mind of winter.
But this much can be certain—
there was truth in the prophetic words
of their coastal cousin, Chief Seattle,
"When the memory of my tribe
shall become a myth . . . at night
when you think your streets deserted
they will throng with returning hosts
who still love this beautiful land.
The white man will never be alone."

And I say to you,
my brothers and my sisters,
that no man we are met this day to honor
shall ever be lost in memory or in myth.
They will ever be a vital part
of the conscience and in the deed
of the great Inland Northwest.
Theirs will be a place
for which tomorrow will make room.
Such is the way of the Inland Northwest.
Such is the stuff of the Vietnam Vet.

II.

It was a long way from Spokane to An Khe.
And longer still from Boise
to the tip of the Southern Cross.
Yet, of all the distances
we were to come to know
the only one without direction
was Death.
And the one which was the farthest still
was the way back home.

They said it was another hemisphere,
but truly it was another world.
And some of us went to be heroes
some of us went to be men
and some of us got to be wondering
some of us got to be dead.
Now, some of us took pungi stakes

somewhere beneath the knee
and some of us stopped psychic bullets
there, right there, between the eyes.
And those of us who could came home
with purple hearts
or purple minds
to a million unfair questions
we could not answer
even to ourselves.

A billion words it seems
and then a billion more
could not explain our war to us
nor change a single lie to truth.
We fought a war in a place
one hundred billion dollars
could not buy a thing worth having
which could not be had
for five hundred piastres.
And when our nation spent it—
our money and our youth,
the monsoons came that year
as they had the past ten thousand.
When it ended there was no peace.
Only the shooting stopped.
Not one mother from either side could say,
"This that we won was worth my son."

And yet not one of us here today,
nor any friend or foe we have, could disagree—
we had fought the finest, light infantry
in the world—
we fought him on his ground
and we beat him into that ground.
No one here ever lost any war He was in!
Nor even a single battle!!

There was just nothing to be won in Vietnam.
There is just nothing any more to be won in
   any war.

III.

These days
the closest we have come to peace
is a brinkmanship at the edge of annihilation.
There is a reason.
And the Vietnam veteran can help correct it.
Today, Vietnam is not a war.
Vietnam is not a place.
Vietnam is a moral question
each man asks on the ledge of his conscience
where he has crawled out to consider his world.
There, above the street of his guilt,
he hears the thousand, thousand catcalls
of mindless opinion
urging him to take that final step
into the empty blackness
of one more war

and debates whether to reenter the open window
of his final reason
to renegotiate the differences
among the family of man
in a world too technically brittle
to permit the continued throwing of rocks
and other missiles.

But at the time we fought it
our war was far more real than spiritual.
Our role far more vital
than the world has ever known . . .
Our war was less in geography than in Time.
Less in politics than in philosophy.
And far less in strategy
than in the evolving collective consciousness
of modern man.

Vietnam existed
somewhere between the last world war
and nuclear holocaust.
Between the unbelievable and the unthinkable.

The veterans of Vietnam
on either side of the war
bought their nations and the world
a generation of Time.
For the fifteen years we fought there
and the twenty-five years
the moral argument has raged in America,
our commitment to a limited war in Vietnam

served to slow and then stop
The Doomsday Clock.
The final hour of unlimited war.
The final moment of mankind
and the world he failed to cherish.
When America honors its war dead from Vietnam
the whole world should bow its head with us.

The only way the sacrifice of the Vietnam veteran
could be for nothing
is if the Time he bought our world meant nothing.
Since our war
The Doomsday Clock ticks on
its seemingly inexorable rhythm
matches the quickening lub-dub
of the human heart—
it is the metronome of nothingness . . .

And still our leaders quibble.

As soldiers and sons
we were obedient,
as veterans and fathers
we must be directive.
It is not enough to memorialize our sacrifice.
We must monumentalize our legacy:
Limited war is futile.
Nuclear war is impossible.
We must amend our living constitution
to include the true cost of war

and the incalculable, higher cost of indifference.
We must continue to share the truth
of our perspective.

IV.

We live on a real world
in a just-right universe
measured in ellipse
shadowed by eclipse
and threatened by the theory
of the Death Star "Nemesis"—
thirteen million miles out
(and closing fast).
Yet, I have neither the inclination
nor the shape of skull to ponder
such enormities.
True to my own nature,
my soul remains simply a Nazi's nightmare.
And yours, I suspect, hates truly the apathy
which allows small children to go hungry.
And yours over there waits only
for that one, calm day
no horseman comes.
And you and I and all our brothers
will jump astride the wind
and chase Johnny's smile
halfway across the universe, hollerin',
"Johnny, we did it! Johnny, we did it!"
Until we catch up to where his laughter waits

beyond the farthest moon
of our most dear dream
just one, last breath
ahead of us all . . .

One hundred years from now
(on the face of the Old Railroad Clock)
when spacecraft made of microchips
and fueled by an exact belief
in the reality of Up,
will circle a world free of slavery
free of war,
and peopled by a mankind
whose concept of humanity travels freely
across all borders of patriotism,
there will come a small child to this place
in the still great, Inland Northwest
who will ask with a pull of her hand,
Who was this man in the bronze statue?
What did he do?
And was he very brave to have done it?

And if you and I
who fought with fists and sticks
and struggled with long division
remain true to our cause to save tomorrow
for all our children,
then the answer to that question
will be the same though it be asked
each day for a thousand years,

"Child, this man was the best of his generation.
He fought very hard in war, to be sure,
but most of all, he fought even harder for peace.
He became his nation's last warrior.
Truly, he was a man who believed in mankind.
Yes, he was a brother to the 'Children of the Sun.' "

Shared at the Peace Memorial, Old Town, San Diego, Memorial Day, 1984

AFTER THE READING OF THE NAMES

I just call him Johnny;
like in Johnny went off to war
and Johnny didn't come home.
And remember him,
like Johnny was a helluva ballplayer
and Johnny's girl believed in dreams.
And I can find him,
like in Johnny's folks
moved away that year—
some say, Minnesota;
but his name's still here
not two miles from his old high school
on a Peace Memorial
(which is a funny name for it).

Sometimes, like today,
we read All the names
some call it "the reading of the names."
Me, I just call it Johnny's Song.
And as much as I love the words,
I've come to really hate the music . . .